Lee Roark

Presented To

Marty Garrett

From

December 1998

Date

COFFEE BREAK WITH GOD

Honor Books
Tulsa, Oklahoma

Coffee Break With God, portable
ISBN 1-56292-506-7
Copyright © 1998 by Honor Books
P.O. Box 55388
Tulsa, Oklahoma 74155

REFERENCES

Unless otherwise indicated, all Scripture quotations are taken from the *Holy Bible, New International Version*® NIV®. Copyright © 1973, 1978, 1984 by International Bible Society. Used by permission of Zondervan Publishing House. All rights reserved.

Scripture quotations marked KJV are taken from the *King James Version* of the Bible.

Scripture quotations marked AMP are taken from *The Amplified Bible, Old Testament*. Copyright © 1965 by Zondervan Publishing House, Grand Rapids, Michigan. *New Testament* copyright © 1958 by The Lockman Foundation, La Habra, California. Used by permission.

Scripture quotations marked NKJV are taken from *The New King James Version* of the Bible. Copyright © 1979, 1980, 1982, 1994 by Thomas Nelson, Inc., Publishers. Used by permission.

Scripture quotations marked NASB are taken from the *New American Standard Bible*. Copyright © 1960, 1962, 1963, 1968, 1971, 1972, 1973, 1975, 1977 by The Lockman Foundation. Used by permission.

Scripture quotations marked RSV are taken from *The Revised Standard Version Bible*, copyright © 1952 by the Division of Christian Education of the Churches of Christ in the United States of America and is used by permission.

INTRODUCTION

"Gimme a break" has been a popular phrase in American culture for more than two decades now. And the fact is now, more than ever, we *need* a break!

A day has a way of pulling us into its wake, almost against our will. Often, our day does not go as planned, and few days go as smoothly as we would like.

However, no matter how frantic the schedule or desperate the situation we can turn to God's Word. There is simply no better break than one that pulls us away from trouble and draws us closer to the Answer, the Lord Jesus Christ.

No one may "give" you a break today. But you can give yourself one. In the *middle* of your day, give yourself a coffee break with God. Allow Him to make whatever course corrections may be necessary for your ultimate and eternal good.

RUNNING PERSISTENTLY

❧ BOB KEMPAINEN was determined to make the 1996 U.S. Men's Olympic marathon team. He was willing to go to any lengths, no matter how gut-wrenching.

On a hilly course in Charlotte, N.C., he won the Trials—but was sick five times in the last two miles.

Kempainen, the American record-holder in the marathon, has experienced stomach troubles since junior high school. But that hasn't kept this medical student from pursuing marathoning.

"To stop was out of the question," he said when asked about his physical condition. With the goal in sight, he knew there would be plenty of time to rest after the race and five months to prepare for Atlanta.

Life is not a level, smooth path, but rather a series of hills and valleys. There are times spent on the mountain top, when everything seems clear and perfect. Then there are those times when we feel like we're wandering around in a dark cavern.

Take a moment and set your heart to be persistent in your faith—faith in God to lead you, pick you up when you have fallen, give you strength to go on, and ultimately bring you to victory. ✑

It is God who arms me with strength and makes my way perfect.
He makes my feet like the feet of a deer; he enables me
to stand on the heights.
—2 SAMUEL 22:33-34

WHAT TO DO

❧ AN ANCIENT Jewish story tells of a young traveler who encountered an old man at the edge of a forest. Staring into the darkness of the overgrown foliage in front of him, the young man asked his elder, "Can you tell me the best way through this forest?"

The wise old man replied, "I cannot."

The young man asked, "But haven't you lived here for awhile? Surely you have been in the forest many times."

"Yes," the old man said, agreeing with both of the young traveler's assumptions. "And I can tell you all of the pitfalls and dangers I have encountered. I can tell you which paths *not* to take. But I have never been all the way through the forest. That is something you must experience for yourself."

Every day, we encounter all kinds of problems which others may have faced before us. The best advice others give us may very well fall into the category of things "not to do."

It is critical therefore, for us to rely upon the counsel of the Lord every hour of the day. He alone knows the precise solution for the particular circumstance we face. ✺

But if any of you lacks wisdom, let him ask of God, who gives to
all men generously and without reproach, and it will be given to him.
—JAMES 1:5 NASB

Staying Charged Up

❧ JUST LIKE a car battery, our energy supply is not infinite. We must replenish it frequently with sleep, rest, food, and relaxation. Our busy, nonstop days can be draining. Operating at top speed, we utilize all available emotional, physical, mental, and spiritual resources. Before we know it, our energy is consumed.

Unless we pay careful attention we will drain our "battery" to the point of feeling "dead on our feet." Being fatigued can distort our perception and cause our responses to others to be negative. It can also result in physical or emotional illness.

Before automatic headlight controls were installed in automobiles, it was easy to park a car and leave the headlights on. If we were gone for very long we returned to find the battery dead. To get the car running again the battery had to be recharged—the car would *not* start until it was!

The age we live in has been described as the age of the to-do list that can't be done. Facing overwhelming demands, it's hard to give ourselves permission to rest or take a break. But the rewards—renewed perspective, clearer insight, physical energy, spiritual preparedness—are well worth it. 🖋

Let the people renew their strength.
—ISAIAH 41:1 KJV

ALONG THE WAY

SCOTTISH EXPLORER Mungo Park made quite a name for himself, though he lived only 35 years in the late 1700s. During his short stay on earth, he managed to have the kind of adventures from which legends are made.

Ernest Hemingway eventually retold one of Park's stories. Park was lost and alone in the African desert and had resigned himself to die. Then he saw it: a beautiful moss-flower. The plant was only as big as one of his fingers, Park said, but he was overcome with admiration for its symmetry.

"Can the Being who planted, watered, and brought to perfection, in this obscure part of the world, a thing which appears of so small importance, look with unconcern upon the situation and suffering of creatures formed after His own image?" he asked. "Surely not."

Thus encouraged, putting aside his hunger and fatigue, Park rose and made his way to relief. We can draw inspiration from his example. He was a man who knew when to push ahead, when to rest, and how to appreciate the simple things in life—and their Creator—along the way. 🖋

See how the lilies of the field grow. They do not labor or spin.
Yet I tell you that not even Solomon in all his splendor
was dressed like one of these.
—MATTHEW 6:28-29

EDITING YOUR LIFE

❧ DISNEY FILMS are known the world over as the best in animation, but the studio didn't earn that reputation easily. One of the reasons for the level of excellence achieved was the filmmaker himself. Walt Disney was ruthless about cutting anything that got in the way of the unfolding story.

Ward Kimball, one of the animators for *Snow White*, recalls working 240 days on a four-minute sequence. The dwarfs made soup for Snow White, almost destroying the kitchen in the process. Disney thought it was funny, but he decided the scene interrupted the flow of the picture, so it was edited out.

Often we find ourselves doing "good" things which are not only unnecessary, but a distraction from the unfolding story of our lives.

As you pause to consider the rest of your day, consider this: when the film of your life is shown, will it be as great as it might have been? A lot will depend on the multitude of *good* things you edit out of your life in favor of the *great* things God wants to do through you! ✍

Wherefore seeing we also are compassed about with so great
a cloud of witnesses, let us lay aside every weight,
and the sin which doth so easily beset us.
—HEBREWS 12:1 KJV

LIFE'S ESSENCE

BEN PATTERSON writes in *The Grand Essentials*:

"Exhibit A is a distant uncle. . . . All his life he did nothing but find new ways to get rich. . . . He spent his senescence very comfortably, drooling and babbling constantly about the money he had made. . . . When life whittled him down to his essence, all there was left was raw greed. This is what he had cultivated in a thousand little ways over a lifetime.

"Exhibit B is my wife's grandmother. . . . When she died in her mid-eighties, she had already been senile for several years. What did this lady talk about? The best example I can think of was when we asked her to pray before dinner. She would reach out and hold the hands of those sitting beside her . . . and her chin would quaver as she poured out her love to Jesus. When life whittled her down to her essence, all there was left was love: love for God and love for others."[1]

When life has whittled you to your essence, whom will you most resemble: the uncle or the grandmother? 🖋

For as he thinketh in his heart, so is he.
—PROVERBS 23:7 KJV

WHAT SHAPE ARE YOU IN?

❧ A MODERN potter once described her craft like this:

"Both my hands shaped this pot. And the place where it actually forms is a place of tension between the pressure applied from the outside and the pressure of the hand on the inside. That's the way my life has been. Sadness and death and misfortune and the love of friends and all the things that happened to me that I didn't even choose. . . . But, there are things I believe in about myself, my faith in God and the love of some friends that worked on the insides of me. My life, like this pot, is the result of what happened on the outside and what was going on inside of me. Life, like this pot, comes to be in places of tension."[2]

Throughout the day we may be buffeted by stress, pulled apart by responsibilities, and pressed by challenges that come at us from the outside. During this break, feed your spirit with Scripture. This will keep you strong, renewed, and restored *within*.

Remember, your inner life gives you the strength you need to become a useful vessel in the household of God. ✣

The inward man is being renewed day by day.
—2 CORINTHIANS 4:16 NKJV

FAULTY ASSUMPTIONS

❧ A TRAVELER at an airport went to a lounge and bought a small package of cookies to eat while she read her newspaper. Gradually, she became aware of a rustling noise. Looking from behind her paper, she was flabbergasted to see a neatly dressed man helping himself to her cookies. Not wanting to make a scene, she leaned over and took a cookie herself.

A minute or two passed, and then she heard more rustling. He was helping himself to another cookie! By this time, they had come to the end of the package.

22

She was angry but didn't dare allow herself to say anything. Then, as if to add insult to injury, the man broke the remaining cookie in two, pushed half across to her, ate the other half, and left.

Still fuming, when her flight was announced, the woman opened her handbag to get her ticket. To her shock, there was her pack of unopened cookies!

It's so easy to make assumptions about what is happening around us. Assumptions are not always wrong, but they are never to be trusted. Choose instead to see other people through God's eyes. He always knows what's going on!

The pride of thine heart hath deceived thee, thou that dwellest in the clefts of the rock, whose habitation is high; that saith in his heart, Who shall bring me down to the ground?
—OBADIAH 1:3 KJV

GIVE IT TO GOD

THERE ONCE was an oyster whose story I tell,
Who found that sand had got under his shell;
Just one little grain, but it gave him much pain,
For oysters have feelings although they're so plain.
Now, did he berate the working of Fate,
Which had led him to such a deplorable state?

24

Did he curse out the government, call for an election?
No; as he lay on the shelf, he said to himself:
"If I cannot remove it, I'll try to improve it."
So the years rolled by as the years always do,
And he came to his ultimate destiny—stew.
And this small grain of sand which had bothered him so,
Was a beautiful pearl, all richly aglow.
Now this tale has a moral—for isn't it grand
What an oyster can do with a morsel of sand;
What couldn't we do if we'd only begin
With all of the things that get under our skin.[3] ⁏

Your sorrow will turn into joy.
—JOHN 16:20 RSV

THE SPICE OF LIFE

⟨⟩ MOST OF us have a routine we follow every morning. There's also a certain routine for our jobs, and another one that takes over after work. Even on the weekends, there are things that must be done.

Have you come to dread another sink full of dishes, another load of laundry, another car to wash, another lawn to mow, another rug to vacuum, or another floor to scrub? Is there any end to the "routine" of life?

There's no getting out of most of those chores. Someone has to keep things clean and running smoothly. The one thing we *can* control is our attitude toward it all.

Rather than emphasizing the "same old," we should remember what the Bible says: "if anyone is in Christ, he is a new creation; the old has gone, the new has come!" (2 Corinthians 5:17) . . . and, "I will give you a new heart and put a new spirit in you" (Ezekiel 36:26).

God never changes, but He loves variety. He wants us to embrace life and keep our eyes open for new possibilities, our minds open to new ideas, our hearts open to new people who cross our path.

Because of the LORD's great love we are not consumed, for his compassions never fail. They are new every morning; great is your faithfulness.
—LAMENTATIONS 3:22-23

HOLD ON!

A LITTLE girl was very nervous at the prospect of her first horseback ride even though she was to be perched behind her grandfather, who was an excellent rider. As her parents helped her onto the horse, she cried, "What do I do? I don't know how to ride a horse! I haven't done this before! What do I do?"

Her grandfather said in reassuring tones, "Don't worry about the horse or about how to ride it. Just hold on to me, darlin', just hold on to me."

What good advice for us when we find ourselves on what we thought was going to be a tired-old-nag sort of day, which turned out to be a bucking-bronco day instead! We need to "just hold on" to our faith in the Lord and stay in the saddle.

One of the foremost ways in which we hold on to the Lord is through constant communication with Him—a continual flow of prayer and praise. We can pray in any place at any time. Even a "thought" prayer turns our will and focus toward the Lord and is evidence that we are putting our trust in Him. ✍

> *Preserve me, O God, for in You I put my trust.*
> —PSALM 16:1 NKJV

THE STILL, SMALL VOICE

❧ EDWIN BOUGHT a new car with lots of bells and whistles—one of which was a voice-warning system. At first, he was amused to hear the soft female voice gently reminding him that he had failed to fasten his seat belt. Hence, he dubbed the voice the "little woman."

One day, he discovered that the little woman was also programmed to remind him he needed to buy gasoline. He decided, however, that he had enough gas to take him at least another 50 miles, so he kept on driving. But in a few minutes, the little lady repeated the warning again—and again—every few minutes until Edwin was ready to scream.

Finally, he'd had all he could take. He pulled to the side of the road, reached under the dash for the appropriate wires, and yanked. *So much for the little woman,* he thought.

Still feeling very self-satisfied for having had the last say, he promptly ran out of gas! Somewhere inside the dashboard, he was almost certain he could hear the laughter of a woman.

God made us with our own warning system—our conscience. Listen to your conscience. It won't steer you wrong! 🪶

> *My conscience is clear, but that does not make me innocent.*
> *It is the Lord who judges me.*
> —1 CORINTHIANS 4:4

THE RETURN ON GIVING

❧ A DROWNING man gestured frantically to a man standing at the edge of a swimming pool. Splashing his way until he was within arm's reach of the side of the pool, the drowning man hollered: "Here, let me give you my hand." The man reached down into the water, took his outstretched hand, and pulled him to safety. Afterward the impromptu lifesaver told the man he had rescued, "I find it unusual that you said 'let me give you my hand' rather than asking me to give you *my* hand."

The rescued man replied, "I work for a charitable organization, sir. I've discovered that people are always more willing to receive than they are to give!"

While the tendency of our human nature may be to receive more than to give, the Gospel tells us giving is actually the most productive way to receive! Whatever we extend to others, give to others, or do for others comes back to us multiplied.

Find ways to give to those around you today. Especially to those who may be in subordinate positions. Freely share information with them and be generous in your praise and encouragement. Give advice on how to do specific tasks more quickly, more efficiently, or with greater quality. You will find that the more you do to help others in their work, the easier your own workload will become. ✒

Give, and it will be given to you: good measure, pressed down, shaken together, and running over.
—LUKE 6:38 NKJV

ANOTHER POINT OF VIEW

ON JULY 15, 1986, Roger Clemens, the sizzling right-hander for the Boston Red Sox, started his first All-Star Game. In the second inning he came to bat, something he hadn't done in years because of the American League's designated-hitter rule. He took a few uncertain practice swings and then looked out at his forbidding opponent, Dwight Gooden, who had won the Cy Young Award the previous year.

Gooden wound up and threw a white-hot fastball that flew right by Clemens. With an embarrassed smile on his face, Clemens stepped out of the box and asked catcher Gary Carter, "Is that what my pitches look like?"

"You bet it is!" replied Carter. Although Clemens quickly struck out, he went on to pitch three perfect innings and was named the game's most valuable player. With a fresh reminder of how overpowering a good fastball is, he later said from that day on he pitched with far greater boldness.

Occasionally we forget the power we have at our disposal when it comes to speaking the Gospel of Jesus Christ. Maybe we need to step to the other side of the plate for a moment to be reminded! 🐉

So we say with confidence, "The LORD is my helper;
I will not be afraid. What can man do to me?"
—HEBREWS 13:6

WITH ATTITUDE

꙳ "TO LOVE what you do and feel that it matters—how could anything be more fun?" asks Katharine Graham. That's what we all desire, isn't it?

Brother Lawrence, the 17th-century Carmelite, found joy in his job washing dishes at the monastery. In the monotony of his routine work he found the opportunity to focus on God and feel his presence.

Modern-day entrepreneurs Ben Cohen and Jerry Greenfield make and sell ice cream with a purpose. The bottom line of Ben & Jerry's Homemade Ice Cream, Inc., is "How much money is left over at the end of the year?" and "How have we improved life in the community?"

"Leftover money" goes to fund Ben & Jerry's Foundation which distributes funds to worthy nonprofit causes. By helping others with their profits, Ben and Jerry put more *meaning* into their ice cream business.

The Scriptures teach that all service ranks the same with God. It is not what you do that is important, but the spirit in which you do it.

If you feel your work is insignificant, ask God to open your eyes! When you do all for Him and to serve others, no task is unimportant! 🍃

> *Whatever you do, do all to the glory of God.*
> —1 CORINTHIANS 10:31 RSV

STARTING OVER

⤬ IMAGINE THAT a natural disaster strikes your town and destroys everyone's home, as well as all the businesses, community services, recreation areas, and houses of worship. The government predicts that it will take nearly a decade to rebuild the town.

That's what happened to Valmeyer, Illinois, during the 1993 Midwest floods. People who had been neighbors for most of their lives, lost everything except their determination to stick together. So they decided to start over and rebuild together—in record time.

38

To accomplish such a monumental task, people had to step away from their normal lives and commit to new tasks.

In this case, a little motivation went a long way. The $22 million project was on course to be completed by the end of 1996—barely three years after the flood. The statement by Helen Keller, "Every day we should do a little more than is required," could have been the motto of the people of Valmeyer. They took that sentiment to heart and rebuilt their town.[4]

Focus on something that is important to you and then map out a strategy for an "extra" touch. ✍

Jesus has been found worthy of greater honor than Moses, just as the builder of a house has greater honor than the house itself. For every house is built by someone, but God is the builder of everything.
—HEBREWS 3:3-4

BALM

IN CENTURIES past, groves of balsam trees were planted on terraces in the hills south of Jerusalem. They were also planted in fields east of the Jordan River, in the area known as Gilead. The sap from the trees was harvested to create a balm that was considered to have great medicinal value. The balm was used especially to treat scorpion stings and snake bites. Since scorpions and snakes abounded in the wilderness regions of Judea, and throughout the Middle East, the balm was extremely valuable.[5]

The "balm of Gilead" has become identified with Jesus. He is the One Who heals our wounds.

Every day holds the potential for us to experience stings and bites, both literal and figurative. While not life-threatening, these "jabs" from the enemy are hurtful nonetheless. How can we apply the balm of Jesus Christ to them?

The foremost way is through praise. As you praise Jesus, you will find the pain associated with an incident or situation soothed.

Any time we find ourselves under attack or wounded, we can turn our minds and hearts to Him with a word, a thought, or a song of praise. ༄

Is there no balm in Gilead, Is there no physician there? Why then is there no recovery For the health of the daughter of my people?
—JEREMIAH 8:22 NKJV

THE GUIDE

ॐ IN *A Slow and Certain Light*, missionary Elisabeth Elliot tells of two adventurers who stopped by her mission station. Loaded heavily with equipment for the rain forest, they sought no advice. They merely asked her to teach them a few phrases of the language so they might converse a bit with the Indians.

Amazed at their temerity, she saw a parallel between these travelers and Christians. She writes: "Sometimes we come to God as the two adventurers came to me—confident and, we think, well-informed and well-equipped. But has it occurred to us that with all our accumulation of stuff, something is missing?"

She suggests that, we often ask God for far too little. "We know what we need—a yes or no answer, please, to a simple question. Or perhaps a road sign. Something quick and easy to point the way. What we really ought to have is the Guide himself. Maps, road signs, a few useful phrases are good things, but infinitely better is someone who has been there before and knows the way."[6]

And we know that all things work together for good to those who love God.
—ROMANS 8:28 NKJV

HOLY HUMOR

IN UMBERTO Eco's novel *The Name of the Rose*, a villainous monk named Jorge poisoned anyone who came upon the one book in the monastery library that suggested that God laughed. Jorge feared if the monks thought God laughed, He would become too familiar to them, too common, and they would lose their awe of Him. Jorge probably never considered the idea that laughter is one of the things that sets us apart as made in *God's* image.

In *Spiritual Fitness*, Doris Donnelly tells us that humor has two elements: an acceptance of life's incongruities and the ability not to take ourselves too seriously. The Christian faith is filled with incongruities—the meek inherit the earth, the simple teach wisdom, death leads to life, a virgin gives birth, a king is born in a stable. Many of life's incongruities are humorous.[7]

You can benefit from laughing. Humor requires a sense of honesty about yourself—without arrogance or false humility. Laughter has been proven to be good for your health. Take time to laugh—it is good for the soul as well as the body. ⌇

He who sits in the heavens shall laugh.
—PSALM 2:4 NKJV

DAY BY DAY

A MOTHER once stopped by her recently-married daughter's home unexpectedly and was promptly greeted with a flood of tears. Alarmed, the mother asked, "What happened, dear?"

Her daughter replied, "It's not what happened, but what keeps happening!"

Even more concerned, the mother asked, "What *keeps* happening?"

The daughter replied, "Every day there are dishes to be washed, meals to be

46

prepared, and lunch to be packed. Every day there is laundry to be done, beds to be made, and the house to be cleaned."

"And?" the mother asked, still unsure as to the nature of the problem. "Don't you see?" the daughter said through her tears. "Life is just so *daily*."

On those days when the "daily-ness" of life seems to have you bogged down in boredom or drudgery, remind yourself the Lord said He would provide for the needs of His people on a daily basis. Manna was gathered in the wilderness every morning. Jesus taught His disciples to pray for their "daily bread." God wants to provide what we need, not only physically and materially, but emotionally and spiritually . . . day by day, one day at a time.

> *Give us this day our daily bread.*
> —MATTHEW 6:11 KJV

ENCUMBRANCES

~ IN JULES Verne's novel, *The Mysterious Island*, he tells of five men who escape a Civil War prison camp by hijacking a hot-air balloon.

As they rise into the air, they realize the wind is carrying them over the ocean. With the surface of the ocean drawing closer, the men decide they must cast some of the weight overboard. Shoes, overcoats, and weapons are reluctantly discarded, and the uncomfortable aviators feel their balloon rise.

However, it isn't long before they find themselves dangerously close to the waves again, so they toss their food overboard. Unfortunately, this too, is only a temporary solution and the craft again threatens to lower the men into the sea. They finally tie the ropes that hold the passenger car and sit on them so they can cut away the basket beneath them. As they do this, the balloon rises again.

Not a minute too soon, they spot land. They are alive because they were able to discern the difference between what was really needed and what was not. The "necessities" they once thought they couldn't live without were the very weights that almost cost them their lives.

Do *you* need to throw anything overboard?

Let us lay aside every weight, and the sin which so easily ensnares us.
—HEBREWS 12:1 NKJV

STOP AND THINK

❧ WHAT IS this life if, full of care,
We have no time to stand and stare.
No time to stand beneath the boughs
And stare as long as sheep or cows.
No time to see, when woods we pass,
Where squirrels hide their nuts in grass.
No time to see, in broad daylight,
Streams full of stars, like stars at night.

No time to turn at Beauty's glance,
And watch her feet, how they can dance.
No time to wait till her mouth can
Enrich that smile her eyes began.
A poor life this if, full of care,
We have no time to stand and stare.[8]

There are two ways of making it through our busy life. One way is to stop thinking. The second is to stop and think. Many people live the first way. They fill every hour with incessant activity. They dare not be alone. There is no time of quiet reflection in their lives.

Throughout the day today, give yourself a five- or ten-minute "mini-vacation." Get alone, be quiet, and listen for God to speak to you. Make time to be alone with God. ✒

God . . . richly furnishes us with everything to enjoy.
—1 TIMOTHY 6:17 RSV

TURNING DARKNESS INTO LIGHT

  ROGER BONE, a physician in Ohio was diagnosed with renal cancer. Surgeons recommended his right kidney and adrenal gland be removed.

After a diagnosis like that, some of us might have isolated ourselves, become bitter and afraid, or tried to deny that anything serious was wrong. Roger Bone teaches us there's a better approach. He says these four observations have become "a way of life" for him.

1. Good health is often taken for granted; however, it is the most precious commodity one possesses.

2. One's spouse, children, family, and friends are the essential ingredients that allow one to endure an experience such as a serious illness.

3. When faced with death, one realizes the importance of God and one's relationship to God.

4. The things one does throughout life that seem so urgent are, most of the time, not so important.[9]

You can come through the fires of your life with the same positive outlook. Begin today by considering what you value most and hold dearest in life. You may be surprised how your priorities change—and how much richer your life becomes. ✒

> *You, O Lord, keep my lamp burning;*
> *my God turns my darkness into light.*
> —Psalm 18:28

A LEATHER-bound COVER

ᐁ DODIE GADIENT, a schoolteacher for thirteen years, decided to travel across America and see the sights she had taught about. Traveling alone in a truck with her camper in tow, she launched out. One afternoon in California's rush-hour traffic, the water pump on her truck blew. She was tired, exasperated, scared, and alone.

Leaning up against the trailer, she finally prayed, "Please God, send me an angel . . . preferably one with mechanical experience." Within four minutes, a huge Harley drove up, ridden by an enormous man. He jumped off, and went to work on the truck.

The intimidated schoolteacher was too dumbfounded to talk—especially when she read the paralyzing words on the back of his leather jacket: "Hell's Angels—California." As he finished the task, she finally got up the courage to say, "Thanks so much," and carry on a brief conversation.

Noticing her surprise at the whole ordeal, he looked her straight in the eye and mumbled, "Don't judge a book by its cover. You may not know who you're talking to." With that he smiled and straddled his Harley. With a wave, he was gone as fast as he had appeared.[10] ✒

For man looketh on the outward appearance,
but the LORD looketh on the heart.
—1 SAMUEL 16:7 KJV

KNOWING YOUR WORTH

∾ IN HIS book, *Up From Slavery*, Booker T. Washington describes an ex-slave from Virginia:

"Two or three years previous to the Emancipation Proclamation, a slave in Virginia made a deal with his master: He was permitted to buy himself, by paying so much per year for his body; and while he was paying for himself, he was permitted to labor where he pleased.

"When freedom came, he was still in debt to his master some 300 dollars. Notwithstanding that the Emancipation Proclamation freed him from any obligation to his master, this black man walked the greater portion of the distance back to where his old master lived in Virginia, and placed the last dollar, with interest, in his hands."[11]

Although he was born into slavery, this man obviously knew his worth. More important, he knew that as a free child of God, his word should be trustworthy. He knew he would sleep peacefully if he kept his word to others.

Be aware of all the promises you make today and be sure to follow through. Not only will you sleep peacefully, but your friends, family, and co-workers will have a new respect for you. ✎

But let your yea be yea; and your nay, nay; lest ye fall into condemnation.
—JAMES 5:12 KJV

PLAYTIME!

A BOY'S HEAD

In it there is a space-ship
and a project for doing away with piano lessons.
And there is Noah's ark
which shall be first.
And there is an entirely new bird,
an entirely new hare,
an entirely new bumble-bee.
There is a river that flows upwards.

> There is a multiplication table.
> There is anti-matter.
> And it just cannot be trimmed.
> I believe that only what cannot be trimmed is a head.
> There is much promise in the circumstance
> that so many people have heads.[12]

Jesus told us we were to *be* like children, not *act* like children! He meant we are to have the unlimited faith and teachability of children. When we are young, everything is new and all situations have the potential for adventure. Even the difficult times are met with a tenacity and courage that we can do whatever is necessary and God will see to it that it will work out fine.

As you take your break today, let God paint new dreams on your heart. Then have the faith of a child and launch out to make them reality. 🖎

Unless you change and become like little children,
you will never enter the kingdom of heaven.
—MATTHEW 18:3

GOD'S PROMISE

❧ GOD HAS not promised to live our lives *for* us—but rather, to walk through our lives *with* us. Our part is to be faithful and obedient. His part is to lead us, guide us, protect us, and help us. Annie Johnson Flint recognized the true nature of God's promise in this poem:

What God Hath Promised

God hath not promised
Skies always blue,
Flower-strewn pathways
All our lives through;

> God hath not promised
> Sun without rain,
> Joy without sorrow,
> Peace without pain.
> But God hath promised
> Strength for the day,
> Rest for the labor,
> Light for the way,
> Grace for the trials,
> Help from above,
> Unfailing sympathy,
> Undying love.[13]

Do what you know you can do today—and then trust God to do what you *cannot* do! ✺

I am with you all the days (perpetually, uniformly, and on every occasion), to the [very] close and consummation of the age.
—MATTHEW 28:20 AMP

MAKING IT TO THE TOP

AFTER BREAKING your back and your ribs, it's very important to stop and regroup. Just ask Jaroslav Rudy.

One day he was riding his motorcycle on a remote trail. While taking a corner a little too fast, he hit a rock and lost control of his bike. Seconds later, he found himself at the bottom of a 30-foot embankment—out of the view of anyone who might be riding or walking on the trail.

For two days, Rudy stayed right where he'd landed, too injured to move.

Freezing temperatures, hunger, and pain finally drove him to try to get back to the trail.

His first attempts were futile—the pain was simply too intense. The next day, after six hours of crawling he reached the trail, where four bicyclists spotted him.

When your strength is gone and there's a goal you simply must achieve, don't give up, but be sensible. Remember to take short breaks along the way—to allow both your creativity and energy to be renewed.

Always remember that no matter how much success you achieve you never do it alone. ✺

Consider it pure joy, my brothers, whenever you face trials of many kinds.
—JAMES 1:2

GIVING ENTRANCE

A RABBI was visited by a number of scholarly men one day. He surprised them by asking, "Where is the dwelling of God?"

The men laughed at him, saying, "What a thing to ask! Is not the whole world full of his glory?"

Then the rabbi answered his own question. "God dwells wherever man lets him in."

When we look at the abundance of problems in our world we can become overwhelmed by the hunger, disease, abuse, crime, etc. Some point to heaven and say, "Where is God? Why doesn't He do something?"

Meanwhile, the Lord is looking at these same situations and crying, "Where are My people? Why don't they do something?"

Perhaps the foremost thing we can do to tackle the problems of our age is this: Invite God into our lives.

When we invite the presence of the Lord into our daily lives we experience His peace and begin to understand how to live according to His plan. We are transformed by His indwelling Holy Spirit into people who manifest morality, kindness, and love. ✍

Behold, I stand at the door and knock; if anyone hears and listens to and heeds My voice and opens the door, I will come in to him and will eat with him, and he [will eat] with Me.
—REVELATION 3:20 AMP

REACHING CONCLUSIONS

≈ TOM MULLEN, in *Laughing Out Loud and Other Religious Experiences*, tells about an engineer, a psychologist, and a theologian who were hunting in the wilds of northern Canada. They came across an isolated cabin and knocked on the door. When no one answered, they entered the cabin. There was nothing unusual about the cabin except that the stove, a large, potbellied one made of cast iron, was suspended in midair by wires attached to the ceiling beams!

"Fascinating," said the psychologist. "It is obvious that this lonely trapper has elevated his stove so he can curl up under it and vicariously experience a return to the womb." The engineer interrupted, "Nonsense! By elevating his stove, he has discovered a way to distribute heat more evenly throughout the cabin."

"With all due respect," said the theologian, "I'm sure that hanging his stove has religious meaning. Fire 'lifted up' has been a religious symbol for centuries." The three debated the point for several minutes and then the trapper returned. When they asked him why he had hung his heavy potbellied stove by wires from the ceiling his answer was succinct: "Had plenty of wire, not much stove pipe!"[14]

But God chose the foolish things of the world to shame the wise;
God chose the weak things of the world to shame the strong.
—1 CORINTHIANS 1:27

SHORTSIGHTED

❧ A FELLOW approached a cab driver in New York and said, "Take me to London." The cab driver told him there was no possible way for him to drive the cab across the Atlantic. The customer insisted there was. "You'll drive me down to the pier and we'll put the taxi on a freighter and when we get off at Liverpool, you'll drive me to London and I'll pay you whatever is on the meter."

The driver agreed and when they arrived in London, the passenger paid the total on the meter, plus a thousand dollar tip.

The driver roamed around London, not quite knowing what to do. Then an Englishman hailed him and said, "I want you to drive me to New York." The cab driver couldn't believe his good luck!

The passenger said, "First, we take a boat . . ." The driver said, "That I know. But where to in New York?" The passenger said, "Riverside Drive and 104th Street."

And the driver responded, "Sorry, I don't go to the west side."[15]

Don't allow your daily routines or shortsightedness to cause you to miss what the Lord wants to do in you and through you. 🖎

As we have therefore opportunity, let us do good unto all men,
especially unto them who are of the household of faith.
—GALATIANS 6:10 KJV

GOD IS GOOD

A SWAN came to rest by the banks of a pond where a crane was hunting snails. The crane eyed the swan and asked, "Where do you come from?"

The swan replied, "I come from heaven!"

"And where is heaven?" asked the crane.

"Heaven!" replied the swan, "Have you never heard of heaven?" And the swan began to describe the splendor of the eternal city. She told the crane about the streets of gold, and the gates and walls made of precious stones. She told about the crystal-clear river of life.

In eloquent language, the swan described the hosts of saints and angels who lived in the world beyond.

Somewhat surprisingly, the crane didn't appear to be the least bit interested in the place the swan described. Eventually he asked the swan, "Are there any snails there?"

"Snails!" declared the swan, obviously revolted. "No! Of course there are not!"

"Then you can have your heaven," said the crane, as it continued its search along the slimy, muddy banks of the pond, "What I want is snails!"[16]

How many of us turn our backs on the good God has for us in order to search for snails? ✍

Friend, go up higher.
—LUKE 14:10 KJV

FRESH BREEZES

❧ WE LIVE our daily lives at such a fast pace these days, we often don't get beyond the most superficial level. James Carroll addressed this tendency, writing:

"We spend most of our time and energy in a kind of horizontal thinking. We move along the surface of things going from one quick base to another, often with a frenzy that wears us out. We collect data, things, people, ideas, and "profound experiences," never penetrating any of them. . . . But there are other times. There

72

are times when we stop. We sit still. We lose ourselves in a pile of leaves or its memory. We listen and breezes from a whole other world begin to whisper."[17]

Perhaps the best thing you can do during your coffee break today is nothing! Shut your office door. Turn off the ringer on the phone. Stare out the window and put your mind and heart into neutral.

Communication with God—prayer—is not just the voicing of praise and petitions, but *communion*. Sitting in silence with God, listening for whatever He may want to say. These special moments with God are when His fresh breezes can enter your heart and refresh you. ✍

I waited patiently and expectantly for the Lord; and He inclined to me.
—PSALM 40:1 AMP

FORM AND SUBSTANCE

A DEVOUT Christian man who had a cat used to spend several minutes each day at prayer and meditation. He cherished this quiet time, but his cat liked it, too. She would cozy up to him, purr loudly, and rub her furry body against him. This interrupted the man's prayer time, so he put a collar around the cat's neck and tied her to the bedpost whenever he wanted to be undisturbed.

When the daughter of this devout Christian began to establish some routines and patterns for her own family, she decided she should do as her father had done. Dutifully, she tied her cat to the bedpost and then proceeded with her devotions. But in her generation, time moved faster and she couldn't spend as much time at prayer as her father did.

The day came when her son was grown up. He also wanted to preserve some of the family tradition. But the pace of life had quickened all the more, so he eliminated devotional time. But in order to carry on the tradition, each day while he was dressing, he tied the family cat to the bedpost!

But thou, when thou prayest, enter into thy closet, and when thou hast shut thy door, pray to thy Father which is in secret; and thy Father which seeth in secret shall reward thee openly.
—MATTHEW 6:6 KJV

WINDOW ON THE WORLD

A LONDON clerk worked in drab surroundings. His office building was in a rundown part of the city.

But that ordinary clerk was not about to let his outlook on life be determined by the dreariness of his surroundings. So one day he bought a beautiful Oriental window painted with an inspiring scene.

The clerk had the window installed high up on the wall in his office. When the hardworking clerk looked through his window, he did not see the familiar slum outside. Instead, he saw a fairy city with beautiful castles, green parks, and lovely homes.

On the window's highest tower there was a large white banner with a strong knight protecting the fair city from a fierce and dangerous dragon. Somehow as he worked long hours at his desk, he felt he was working for the knight on the banner. This feeling produced a sense of honor and dignity. He had found a noble purpose helping the knight keep the city happy, prosperous, and strong.

You don't have to let your circumstances or surroundings discourage you. You are a worker in God's kingdom to bring His beauty to every life around you. ஃ

O LORD, I pray, open his eyes that he may see.
—2 KINGS 6:17 NASB

STAY IN THE GAME

IN PHILADELPHIA on February 17, 1996, man defeated computer in an internationally-observed classical chess match.

Garry Kasparov, world chess champ, lost the first of the six games to Deep Blue, the IBM super-computer. It was just what he needed, however, because it forced him to pay even closer attention, devise more intricate strategies, and learn more about a game in which he is an acknowledged expert.

Kasparov notched three wins of his own and two draws in the remaining five games of the week-long match. It took every bit of chess knowledge he possessed —and some he developed along the way—to defeat a computer that is capable of calculating fifty billion positions in just three minutes.

When you have to face a "challenger" who seems to outweigh you, have confidence in your abilities, study and practice, and most importantly—pray!

On "game day," relax. Let all the information you've stored in your brain rise to the top. Expect the unexpected and be ready to improvise and make midcourse adjustments as needed. And, save a little something for the next game! ✍

To him who overcomes, I will give the right to sit with me on my throne, just as I overcame and sat down with my Father on his throne.
—REVELATION 3:21

THE TROUBLE WITH BEING RIGHT

A PASSENGER on a dining car looked over the luncheon menu, which included both a chicken salad sandwich and a chicken sandwich. He decided on the chicken salad sandwich, but absent-mindedly wrote chicken sandwich on the order slip. When the waiter brought the chicken sandwich the customer angrily protested.

Instead of picking up the order slip and showing the customer that it was his mistake, the waiter expressed regret at the error, picked up the chicken sandwich, and returned a moment later with a chicken salad sandwich.

While eating his sandwich, the customer picked up the order slip and saw that the mistake was his. When it came time to pay the check the man apologized to the waiter and offered to pay for both sandwiches. The waiter's response was, "No, sir. That's perfectly all right. I'm just happy you've forgiven me for being right."

By taking the blame, the waiter allowed the passenger to retain his dignity, reminded him to be more cautious before blaming others, and created a better atmosphere for everyone in the dining car.

Next time someone blames you for their mistake, don't get defensive. Find a creative way to make things right. ✍

> *Take heed to yourselves: If thy brother trespass against thee,*
> *rebuke him; and if he repent, forgive him.*
> —LUKE 17:3 KJV

WORRY IS A RAT

∼ YEARS AGO, a pilot was making a flight around the world. When he was about two hours away from his last landing field, he heard a noise in his plane which he recognized as the gnawing of a rat. For all he knew the rat could be gnawing through a vital cable. It was a very serious situation. At first he did not know what to do. It was two hours back to the landing field from which he had taken off and more than two hours to the next field.

Then he remembered that the rat is a rodent. It is not made for the heights; it is made to live on the ground. Therefore the pilot began to climb. At about twenty thousand feet the gnawing ceased. The rat was dead.

More than two hours later the pilot brought the plane safely to the next landing field and found the dead rat.

Worry is a rodent. It cannot live in the secret place of the Most High. It cannot breathe in the atmosphere made vital by prayer and familiarity with Scripture. Worry dies when we ascend to the Lord through prayer and His Word.

Who of you by worrying can add a single hour to his life?
—LUKE 12:25

PRAYER PAUSE

🐚 A COFFEE break is a good time for prayer! Try this prayer of St. Patrick:

May the wisdom of God instruct me, the eye of God watch over me, the ear of God hear me, the word of God give me sweet talk, the hand of God defend me, the way of God guide me.

> Christ be with me.
> Christ before me.
> Christ in me.
> Christ under me.

Christ over me.
Christ on my right hand.
Christ on my left hand.
Christ on this side.
Christ on that side.
Christ in the head of everyone to whom I speak.
Christ in the mouth of every person who speaks to me.
Christ in the eye of every person who looks upon me.
Christ in the ear of everyone who hears me today.
Amen.[18]

Take time in the middle of your day to ask the Lord for His wraparound presence, His unending encouragement, and His all-sustaining assistance. And be a vessel that carries His presence, encouragement, and assistance to others. ✍

Uphold me according to Your promise, that I may live.
—PSALM 119:116 AMP

CAN-DO ATTITUDE

WATCH YOUR Can't's and Can's
If you would have some worthwhile plans
You've got to watch your can't's and can's;
You can't aim low and then rise high;
You can't succeed if you don't try;
You can't go wrong and come out right;
You can't love sin and walk in the light;
You can't throw time and means away
And live sublime from day to day.
You can be great if you'll be good
And do God's will as all men should;

86

You can ascend life's upward road,
Although you bear a heavy load;
You can be honest, truthful, clean,
By turning from the low and mean;
You can uplift the souls of men
By words and deeds, or by your pen.
So watch your can't and watch your can's.
And watch your walks and watch your stands,
And watch the way you talk and act,
And do not take the false for fact;
And watch the things that mar or make;
For life is great to every man
Who lives to do the best he can.[19]

Choose to have an "I can" attitude today, and then pursue excellence with all your ability.

And Jesus said unto him, No man, having put his hand
to the plough, and looking back, is fit for the kingdom of God.
—LUKE 9:62 KJV

WHO'S WATCHING?

∼ A MAN named Roy had been a kidnapper and holdup man for twelve years, but while in prison he heard the Gospel and invited Jesus Christ into his life: "Christ said to me, 'I will come and live in you and we will serve this sentence together.' And we did."

Several years later he was paroled, and just before he went out he was handed a letter written by another prisoner, which said "You know perfectly well that when I came into the jail I despised anything that smacked of Christianity.

"Then they told me you were saved, and I said, 'There's another fellow taking the Gospel road to get parole.' But, Roy, I've been watching you for two-and-a-half years. Now I'm a Christian, too, because I watched you. The Saviour [sic] who saved you has saved me. You never made a slip."

Roy says, "When I read that letter I came out in a cold sweat. Think of what it would have meant if I had slipped, even once."[20]

Who might be secretly watching you? A coworker, a child, a boss, or a spouse who needs to know Jesus? You are His representative to that person. ✺

That ye would walk worthy of God,
who hath called you unto his kingdom and glory.
—1 THESSALONIANS 2:12 KJV

STAY INVOLVED

COMEDIAN GEORGE Burns said the clue to happiness is helping others: "If you were to go around asking people what would make them happier, you'd get answers like a new car, a bigger house, a raise in pay, winning a lottery, a face-lift, more kids, less kids, a new restaurant to go to—probably not one in a hundred would say a chance to help people. And yet that may bring the most happiness of all.

"I don't know Dr. Jonas Salk, but after what he's done for us with his polio vaccine, if he isn't happy, he should have that brilliant head of his examined. Of course, not all of us can do what he did. I know I can't do what he did; he beat me to it.

"But the point is, it doesn't have to be anything that extraordinary. It can be working for a worthy cause, performing a needed service, or just doing something that helps another person."[21]

Be imaginative and creative in your deeds of kindness. On those bad days when nothing seems to go right . . . *you* can contribute something "right!" ✒

Trust in the LORD and do good.
—PSALM 37:3 KJV

ACCEPTING SUBSTITUTES

AFTER MOVING to a small town in Wyoming, a woman found that clothing stores were in short supply. To solve her problem, she began relying on a major store catalog. The order forms sent by the store had this sentence printed at the bottom: "If we do not have the article you ordered in stock, may we substitute?"

Since she rarely ordered unless she really needed the article in question, she was hesitant to trust strangers to make an appropriate substitution. But she replied "yes" hoping that substitution wouldn't be necessary.

However, one day she opened a package from the company and found a letter which read, in part, "We are sorry that the article you ordered is out of stock, but we have substituted . . ." When she unwrapped the merchandise she found an article of greater quality worth double the price she paid!

When we pray to God, we are wise to add to our requests that we are quite willing to accept a substitution for what we think we need. Every time He sends "substitutes," we can be sure He is sending something much better than we could have ever imagined. ༄

Now unto him that is able to do exceeding abundantly above all that we ask or think, according to the power that worketh in us.
—Ephesians 3:20 kjv

WHAT NATURE?

∼ THE FOLLOWING prayer by Danish theologian Sören Kierkegaard provides a wonderful word picture of God:

"Father in Heaven, when the thought of thee wakes in our hearts, let it not awaken like a frightened bird that flies about in dismay, but like a child waking from its sleep with a heavenly smile."

The way we regard God has a direct impact on how we pray, and also upon how we treat others. If we see God as a stern Judge, we tend to become more judgmental and less forgiving, even to ourselves.

If we see God as distant and remote, we are likely to dismiss Him from our lives completely, and turn to other people for soul satisfaction—a practice that is likely to leave us feeling empty inside.

However, if we believe in God as our loving, generous, Heavenly Father, we are much more likely to communicate with Him about *everything* we face in life. We are also much more willing to communicate with others and to accommodate their frailties and faults.

In the end, every aspect of our lives—including work—is impacted by the nature of our relationship with God.

How *do* you regard God? ✍

> *The LORD is my Shepherd . . . only goodness, mercy,*
> *and unfailing love shall follow me all the days of my life.*
> —PSALM 23:1,6 AMP

ON CALL

 TODAY'S COMMUNICATIONS technology gives immediate access to anyone, virtually anywhere. Therefore, we seldom "get away from it all."

Because of that phenomenon, Dr. Mark Moskowitz of Boston University's Medical Center observes, "A lot of people are working 24 hours a day, seven days a week, even when they're not technically at work." That is a precursor to first-class exhaustion.

Government executive Roy Neel quit his job as deputy chief of staff in the Clinton Administration when he realized that work "even for the president of the United States" is not worth the price. One night Roy and his 9-year-old son Walter were ready to walk out the door for a long-promised baseball game and the phone rang. It was the president. Walter was not impressed by a call from the White House, what he wanted was to go to a baseball game with his dad. After the hour-long phone call, Neel discovered his son had found a ride to the game with a neighbor. Neel says, "Our society has become schizophrenic. We praise people who want balance in their lives, but reward those who work themselves to death."[22]

Remember what "all work and no play" did to Jack? 🖎

O that I had wings like a dove! I would fly away and be at rest.
—PSALM 55:6 RSV

KNOWING GOD'S WILL

ST. IGNATIUS of Loyola saw the doing of God's will as not only our command in life, but also our reward:

"Teach us, good Lord, to serve thee as thou deservest: to give and not to count the cost; to fight and not to heed the wounds; to toil and not to seek for rest; to labor and not to ask for any reward save that of knowing that we do thy will."[23]

It is as we know we are doing God's will that we find true meaning in life and a deep soul-satisfying sense of accomplishment and purpose.

But how can we know that we are doing God's will?

First, commit yourself to the Lord each day by simply saying, "Lord, I put my life in Your hands. Do with me what You will."

And second, trust the Lord to send you the work and the relationships you need for His purpose in your life to be accomplished.

As Roberta Hromas, a noted Bible teacher once said: "Simply answer your door, answer your phone, and answer your mail. The Lord will put in your path the opportunities that He desires for you to pursue."

> *Now therefore, I pray You, if I have found*
> *favor in Your sight, show me now Your way.*
> —EXODUS 33:13 AMP

A QUIET MOMENT

BETWEEN THE great issues of life there is quiet. Silence characterizes the highest in art and the deepest in nature. It's the silence between the notes that give them rhythm, interest, and emphasis.

Silence reaches beyond words. The highest point in drama is silence. The most valid emotions don't always cry aloud. The sincerest sympathy is not wordy. The best planning for an emergency is the calm of quietness.

Time spent in quiet prayer is the best preparation for intelligent action. The best indicator of confidence is almost always silence. The person who is confident of her position does not argue or try to explain everything.

Quiet times are most cherished in the middle of busy days. Sometimes the quiet does not offer itself; it must be sought out. At other times, the surroundings don't allow for true silence. It is in those moments when the Holy Spirit can supernaturally turn down the volume and allow moments of quiet communion with God from within.

A coffee break is a perfect time to seek a quiet spot for a few minutes of real refreshment in the presence of a "still, small voice" (1 Kings 19:12 KJV).

For thus saith the Lord GOD, the Holy One of Israel; In returning and rest shall ye be saved; in quietness and in confidence shall be your strength.
—ISAIAH 30:15 KJV

A KITE'S TALE

ONE SUNDAY, a pastor told the little ones this story:

On a breezy March day, the town mayor happened through the park where a small boy was flying the largest, most beautiful kite he had ever seen. It soared so high, the mayor was sure it must be visible from the next town. Since his little town did not have very many things of note to its credit, the mayor decided to reward the one responsible for setting this spectacle aloft.

"Who is responsible for flying this kite?" the mayor inquired.

"I am," said the boy. "I made the kite with my own hands. I fly the kite," he declared.

"I am," said the wind. "It is my whim that keeps it aloft and sets the direction it will go. I fly the kite," the wind cooed.

"Not so," exclaimed the kite's tail. "I make it sail and give it stability against the wind's whims. I fly the kite," declared the tail.

Now who flies the kite?—the pastor asked.

"They all do!" said several kids in concert. Smart kids!

The next time you pass one of your coworkers in the hall, tell them you're glad they are part of the team! ✍

> *Just as each of us has one body with many members,*
> *and these members do not all have the same function.*
> —ROMANS 12:4

WHAT A FRIEND!

  JOSEPH SCRIVEN, the writer of the hymn "What a Friend We Have in Jesus," had a life of great sorrow. A day or two before their wedding, his fiancee drowned. This tragedy put him into a melancholy that stayed with him the rest of his life.

In spite of his despondent temperament, the power and presence of God were evident in Scriven's life. He was a philanthropist and a devout Christian. He had a reputation as the man "who saws wood for poor widows and sick people who are unable to pay." To other people Scriven *was* the friend that they had found in Jesus.

Scriven wrote this hymn to comfort his mother in a time of sorrow in her own life. He never intended that anyone else see it, but the manuscript was discovered by a neighbor. When asked later if he had written it, Scriven said, "The Lord and I did it between us."[24]

Jesus didn't die for you so you could go through struggles alone and carry heavy burdens by yourself. He gave Himself so you and He could become friends, and friends always stand by and help each other.

> *I have called you friends.*
> —JOHN 15:15 RSV

WHATSOEVER THINGS ARE JUST

❧ GEORGE F.R. ELLIS is a well-known cosmologist. On his "day job," he evaluates and devises theories concerning the origin and structure of the universe. His "calling," however, is to identify and eliminate injustice where he finds it.

Growing up in Johannesburg, South Africa, Ellis observed plenty of injustice. His father lost his newspaper job for criticizing the government. His mother helped found a group of white women voters who spent forty years fighting apartheid.

After Ellis left home to study at the University of Cambridge, he joined the Society of Friends (Quakers) and embraced their rational, nonviolent ways. He returned to South Africa to teach, and to see what he could do about bringing an end to apartheid.

Ellis helped raise money to set up an orphanage and a program to distribute milk. He devised a basic housing plan for the needy and publicized evidence concerning the government's "undeclared war" against blacks.[25]

British statesman and political thinker Edmund Burke once said, "The only thing necessary for the triumph of evil is for good men to do nothing." Like George F.R. Ellis, when we take such ideas to heart we are putting ourselves in position to become world-changers. ✎

Woe to those who enact evil statutes, And to those who constantly record unjust decisions, So as to deprive the needy of justice, And rob the poor of My people of their rights.
—ISAIAH 10:1-2 NASB

NOT WORTH A DIME

❧ A YOUNG man was invited to preach at a church in Nashville, Tennessee. On an impulse he used as his text, "Thou shalt not steal."

The next morning he stepped onto a city bus and handed the driver a dollar bill. The driver handed him back his change and he walked to the rear of the bus.

When he counted his change there was a dime too much. His first thought was, *The bus company will never miss this dime.*

By now the bus had stopped again and the narrow aisle between him and the driver was one long line of people. Then it hit him, he could not keep money that did not belong to him.

A half dozen "excuse me's" and several scowling looks later, he had made his way to the front and said to the driver, "You gave me too much change."

The driver replied, "Yes, a dime too much. I gave it to you on purpose. You see, I heard your sermon yesterday, and I watched in my mirror as you counted your change. Had you kept the dime I would never again have had any confidence in preaching."

Our influence is like a shadow; it may fall even where we think we've never been. ✒

> *There is nothing concealed that will not be disclosed,*
> *or hidden that will not be made known.*
> —LUKE 12:2

SIGNPOSTS

 ONE VERY dark night a man drove along a deserted road on his way to a place he had visited only once before. As he drove, he suddenly became uneasy, thinking he might have missed a turn two or three miles back.

He drove on mile after mile. Several times he slowed down, overcome by indecision. If he was wrong, turning back would cost him an additional twenty or thirty minutes and he was barely on schedule as it was.

Slower and slower he went. He began to think, "Even if it's a mistake, I have to go back to reassure myself."

Just as he was about to turn around, his headlights reflected off a white marker in the distance. He increased his speed and soon saw the familiar shield that marks U.S. highways. The number 82 was clearly visible, and that was the road he needed to take. He continued on his way with confidence.

Sometimes in the dark nights of our travel through life, we feel we've missed a turn or read a sign incorrectly. Knowing our indecision, God gives us reassuring signs to help us reestablish our heading and our confidence. 🪶

When my spirit was overwhelmed within me, then thou knewest my path.
—PSALM 142:3 KJV

RISE GENTLY AND SLOWLY

❧ SCUBA DIVING is a sport that grows more and more popular every year. But those who take it up must be aware of the dangers it poses.

One of the biggest threats is decompression illness, or "the bends." While divers are underwater, they breathe compressed air; its pressure is equal to that of the water around them. If the diver stays down a long time and dives deeply, his body absorbs a great deal of compressed gas. If he then ascends too quickly, his body can't expel the extra gases slowly enough to avoid the formation of bubbles in his body tissues.

Divers suffering from decompression must be recompressed in a hyperbaric chamber, and then gradually decompressed while breathing pure oxygen.

How can decompression be avoided? By ascending more slowly, with several interruptions along the way. Another method is taking a "safety stop" for several minutes at a depth of five or six meters.[26]

When it comes to our career, how quickly do we want to rise to the top? Is it worth getting "the bends" to arrive there faster than anyone else? ✍

So teach us to number our days,
That we may present to Thee a heart of wisdom.
—PSALM 90:12 NASB

MOMENTS OF CONTENTMENT

WHEN STRESSFUL situations attempt to rob us of our peace, we need to ask the Lord to renew His presence within us. This prayer by Louis Bromfield seems to have been written for just those times:

"Oh, Lord, I thank you for the privilege and gift of living in a world filled with beauty and excitement and variety.

"I thank you for the gift of loving and being loved, for the friendliness and understanding and beauty of the animals on the farm and in the forest and marshes, for the green of the trees, the sound of a waterfall, the darting beauty of the trout in the brook.

"I thank you for the delights of music and children, of other men's thoughts and conversation and their books to read by the fireside or in bed with the rain falling on the roof or the snow blowing past outside the window."[27]

You may not be in a place where you have great beauty around you, but you can close your eyes and imagine yourself in such a place. Make that secret chamber of your heart your place of prayer. Your place to experience contentment. ✒

I have learned how to be content (satisfied to the point where
I am not disturbed or disquieted) in whatever state I am.
—PHILIPPIANS 4:11 AMP

SMALL THINGS

IN A certain bank there was a trust department in which four young men and one older man were employed. The directors decided to promote the older employee and promote one of the younger men to take his place in charge of the trust department.

After considering the merits of each of the young men, the directors selected one of them for the new position. They decided to notify him of the promotion that afternoon at four o'clock.

During the noon hour the young man went to a cafeteria for lunch. One of the directors was behind him in line, with several other customers in between them. The director saw the young man select his food, including a piece of butter, which he hid under his other food.

That afternoon the directors met to notify the young man that they had intended to give him the promotion, but because of what had been seen in the cafeteria, they told him they must discharge him instead.

The next time you are tempted to "borrow" something from your employer, picture Jesus asking you where you got it! ✍

> *He that is faithful in that which is least is faithful also in much:*
> *and he that is unjust in the least is unjust also in much.*
> —LUKE 16:10 KJV

HIS WAY

 ONE SPRING a wild duck was flying north across the European continent. On the flight he stopped in a barnyard, where some ducks were being raised for food. Enjoying the food and security of the barnyard, he decided to stay for an hour, then a day, then a week, then a month, and finally all summer.

Summer eventually turned to autumn and his wild duck friends, heading south for the winter, flew overhead. He flapped his wings to fly up and join his friends, but he quickly found that the delicious fare he had enjoyed all summer had made him so soft and heavy he could not fly any higher than the roof of the barn.

Every spring, and then again every autumn, he heard the honking of the wild ducks as they flew over the barnyard. For a few seasons, he tried to join his mates, but the day finally came when the barnyard duck paid no attention to the wild ducks honking and flying overhead.

If we get sidetracked just as the wild duck did, we need to draw near to God. Like a magnet that has been demagnetized and has lost its ability to determine direction, we can get back on track by staying in close contact with the most powerful magnet in the universe, Jesus Christ. He never loses His sense of direction! ✣

> *May the Lord direct your hearts into the love of God*
> *and into the steadfastness of Christ.*
> —2 THESSALONIANS 3:5 NASB

119

THEY ALREADY KNEW HIM

 A MISSIONARY was sent to a faraway land where few Westerners had ever ventured. To anyone's knowledge, no missionary had ever ministered in that area.

Having painstakingly learned the language, the missionary gathered the village together to hear their first sermon about a loving God. He told of the selfless love, infinite compassion, merciful tenderness, and dynamic healing power of Christ. He was pleased to see how interested the crowd was.

Then he noticed they were beginning to nod and smile knowingly, as if they already knew the Man who went about doing good. He asked how many of them had ever heard of this Man.

The response was overwhelming. It seemed they all knew Him! Astonished, he asked, "How? When? Who told you about Him?"

"He used to live among us!" an older gentleman said. "We called him Doctor, but he was as you've described him exactly."

As it turned out, the village had once had the services of a Christian physician who lived among them and took care of them for many years. So strong was his simple, Christ-like love and caring that the villagers had mistaken him for the Savior the missionary described.

Determine to live your life in such a way that even the lost would recognize Jesus in you! 🐿

Let your light so shine before men, that they may see your good works, and glorify your Father which is in heaven.
—MATTHEW 5:16 KJV

THE EMPTY TOMB

◆ PHILIP WAS born a Mongoloid. He was a happy child, but as he grew older he became increasingly aware that he was different. He went to Sunday school with boys and girls his own age, but he was treated as an outsider.

As an Easter lesson, each child was to find something that symbolized new life to them, put it in a plastic egg, and bring it back to share with the class.

When they gathered back in the classroom, they put their eggs on the table, and watched with great anticipation as the teacher opened each egg. In one egg, there was a flower, in another a butterfly.

When teacher opened the next egg there was nothing in it. Philip went up to the teacher, tugged on her sleeve, and said, "It's mine." The children laughed and said, "You never do anything right, Philip. There's nothing there."

Philip replied, "I did so do it. I *did* do it. It's empty—the tomb is empty!"

The classroom fell silent. And from that day on things were different. Philip had been freed from the tomb of his being different and given a new life among his peers.[28] ॐ

> *Be honest in your judgment and do not decide at a glance*
> *(superficially and by appearances); but judge fairly and righteously.*
> —JOHN 7:24 AMP

THE RIPPLE EFFECT

A CENTURY and a half ago a humble minister lived and died in a small village in Leicestershire, England. He had lived there all his life and never traveled far from home.

In his congregation was a young cobbler to whom he gave special attention, teaching him the Word of God. This young man was William Carey, later hailed as one of the greatest missionaries of modern times.

This same minister had a son—a boy whom he taught faithfully and constantly encouraged. The boy's character and talents were profoundly impacted by his father's life. That son grew up to be a man many considered the mightiest public orator of his day: Robert Hall.

It seems the village pastor accomplished little in his life as a preacher. There were no spectacular revivals, great miracles, or church growth spurts. But his faithful witness and godly life had much to do with giving India its Carey and England its Robert Hall.

When you think you are having no impact in the world, remember the little country preacher who influenced two nations for the Lord. ✍

Which indeed is the least of all seeds: but when it is grown,
it is the greatest among herbs, and becometh a tree,
so that the birds of the air come and lodge in the branches thereof.
—MATTHEW 13:32 KJV

125

Come On Up

ICE CLIMBING is perhaps the most dangerous specialty in mountain climbing, but some climbers *choose* to do it!

Every ice climber wears crampons, a steel frame with spikes that straps to their boots. The first thing prospective climbers learn is to move from side to side on an ice wall while wearing crampons. Then next comes technique. Each style applies to a different phase of the climb.

Some walls have a lower-grade pitch—twenty to thirty degrees. The greater the pitch, the more difficult the climb. At ninety degrees, a climber has to haul himself up with his whole body.

Ice climbers also wear a safety harness with one end of a rope threaded through it. The other end of the rope is fastened securely at the top of the wall, where other team members anticipate a fall and take some of the slack out of the rope—preventing serious injuries to the climber.[29]

Isn't that how it is in many endeavors? We think we only need to use one technique or that our strength alone will help us get by. Then we realize we must pray, study God's Word, and learn to lean on other believers from time to time. ✺

After many days had gone by, the Jews conspired to kill him,
but Saul learned of their plan. Day and night they kept close watch
on the city gates in order to kill him. But his followers took him by night
and lowered him in a basket through an opening in the wall.
—ACTS 9:23-25

EXPERTISE

◆ THE STORY is told of a postgraduate student who went to the great naturalist Agassiz to receive the finishing touches on his education. Expecting a noble assignment, he was surprised when Agassiz gave him a small fish and told him to describe it.

Within a few minutes the student returned with the description of the fish according to formal Latin terminology, and provided the genus and family in which the fish might be found on a chart. Agassiz read what the student had written and then said, "Describe the fish for me."

The student then produced a four-page essay. Agassiz again told him to look at the fish and describe it. This continued for three weeks, but the student had to admit, by then he really *knew* something about the fish. And Agassiz agreed.[30]

One modern-day philosopher has concluded that if you were to study only one small item, plant, or creature for five minutes a day for the next twenty years, you would be the world's foremost expert on that subject!

How important it is, then, that we spend time every day learning the most important lessons of all—those found in God's Word. ✍

Study and be eager and do your utmost to present yourself to God approved
(tested by trial), a workman who has no cause to be ashamed,
correctly analyzing and accurately dividing [rightly
handling and skillfully teaching] the Word of Truth.
—2 TIMOTHY 2:15 AMP

DO-IT-YOURSELF MISERY

HERE'S A sure-fire recipe for misery printed in *The Gospel Herald*:

> Think about yourself.
> Talk about yourself.
> Use "I" as often as possible.
> Be suspicious.
> Expect to be appreciated.
> Be jealous and envious.
> Be sensitive to slights.
> Never forgive a criticism.

Trust nobody but yourself.
Insist on consideration and the proper respect.
Demand agreement with your own views on everything.
Never forget a service you may have rendered.
Be on the lookout for a good time for yourself.
Shirk your duties if you can.
Do as little as possible for others.
Love yourself supremely.
Be selfish.[31]

This recipe is guaranteed to work; in fact, you don't even need all the ingredients to achieve total misery.

On the other hand, if misery's not your cup of tea, do just the opposite and you'll have a hard time feeling even a little blue! ꙮ

Deceit is in the heart of them that imagine evil:
but to the counsellors of peace is joy.
—PROVERBS 12:20 KJV

WHEN LIFE HAS BECOME ROUTINE

SOME DAYS seem absent of purpose and motivation. On such a day, you might feel as this man felt:

"When I woke up this morning, I said to myself that this would be a day just like every other day. And it was. I took the same train as every morning, I read the same comments in the paper on an international situation which never changes. On my desk I found the same piles of papers to go through.

"The people all look the same and so does my supervisor. They all had that blank expression which says that nothing new is going to happen today. For lunch I had the same old thing to eat. I went back to my desk until five o'clock. And then I just came home, knowing full well that tomorrow it will start all over again.

"God, I'm tired of it all. I had hoped for something completely different. I had dreamed that some day I would lead an active and exciting life. I'll never be anything but what I am. That was a dream."

To defeat fatigue, boredom, and depression, turn immediately to the Lord for a change of attitude, strength, and wisdom. 🖋

Come unto me, all ye that labour and are heavy laden.
—MATTHEW 11:28 KJV

"FUSSING" AWAY TIME

EARNEST WORKER tells of a dear old lady from the country who went for the first time on a railway journey of about fifty miles through an interesting and beautiful region. She had looked forward to this trip with great pleasure. But it took her so long to get her baskets and parcels right, to get her skirt adjusted, her seat comfortably arranged, the shades and shutters right, that she was just settling down to enjoy the trip when they called out the name of her station!

"Oh my!" she said, "if I had only known that we would be there so soon I wouldn't have wasted my time in fussing. I hardly saw the scenery!"

Continuing to "fuss" with things left behind in yesterday and things yet to do tomorrow robs us of the joys God brings to us today. It makes us constantly "busy" —but not always with the things that will bring lasting joy and meaning into our lives and the lives of those around us. If you've said, "I'm too busy to . . ." several times today, it might be time to review your priorities. ✒

> *Therefore do not worry about tomorrow, for tomorrow will*
> *worry about itself. Each day has enough trouble of its own.*
> —MATTHEW 6:34

GIVE ME A WORD

✏ MARJORIE HOLMES writes in *Lord, Let Me Love*, about her daughter, who had a fascination with words at a young age. From her earliest attempts at talking, she liked to try out new words and sounds.

She was impatient, however, because all the things she was learning at her young age far exceeded her ability to express them. So because she needed more words, she began asking her mother for words, just like she might ask her for a cookie or a hug.

The little girl would ask, "Give me a bright word, Mother." And Marjorie would answer with a string of nouns and adjectives that described the word *bright*, such as "sunshine, golden, luminous, shiny, sparkling." Then she would ask for a soft word. And Marjorie responded, "Velvety soft like a blackberry or a pony's nose. Or furry, like your kitten. Or how about a lullaby?" And when she was angry, she would demand a glad word.[32]

What word do you need today? Do you need a glad word or a comforting word? "Give me a word," can be the prayer of your heart to God.

And the Word was God.
—JOHN 1:1 NKJV

SO SEND I YOU

❧ MARGARET CLARKSON was a 23-year-old school teacher in a gold-mining town in northern Ontario, Canada—far from friends and family. As she meditated on John 20:21 one evening, God spoke to her through the phrase "So send I you." She realized that this lonely area was the place to which "God had sent her." This was her mission field. As she quickly set down her thoughts in verse, one of the most popular missionary hymns of the twentieth century was born:

So send I you to labor unrewarded,
To serve unpaid, unloved, unsought, unknown,
To bear rebuke, to suffer scorn and scoffing—
So send I you to suffer for My sake.
So send I you to bind the bruised and broken,
O'er wand'ring souls to work, to weep, to wake,
To bear the burdens of a world a-weary—
So send I you to suffer for My sake.
". . . So send I you to hearts made hard by hatred,
To eyes made blind because they will not see,
To spend—tho' it be blood—to spend and spare not—
So send I you to taste of Calvary.[33]
"As the Father hath sent Me, so send I you" (John 20:21). ✍

I heard the voice of the Lord, saying, Whom shall I send,
and who will go for us? Then said I, Here am I; send me.
—ISAIAH 6:8 KJV

SOWING PEACE

❧ HEINZ WAS an eleven-year-old Jewish boy who lived with his family in the Bavarian village of Furth during the 1930s. When Hitler's band of thugs came tearing through the village, recreational activities were forbidden, and Furth's streets became a battleground.

One day, Heinz couldn't avoid a face-to-face encounter with a Hitler bully. A brutal beating seemed inevitable. But Heinz walked away from the fray without a scratch. This time he didn't use his fists to fight back, he spoke up instead. He used his persuasive abilities to convince his potential attackers that a fight was not necessary. Heinz used his language skills to avoid battle. This would not be the last time this young Jewish boy would use his peacemaking skill in Hitler-occupied Europe.

Eventually Heinz and his family escaped to America where Heinz would one day make his mark. Throughout the world he became known as a mediator and a peacemaker among world leaders and nations. The young boy who grew up as Heinz, anglicized his name when he came to America. We know him as Henry Kissinger.

Today, put your talents to use as a peacemaker. When you sow seeds of peace you are doing God's work on earth and you will reap a harvest of goodness. ॐ

Blessed are the peacemakers, for they shall be called sons of God.
—MATTHEW 5:9 RSV

KEEP IT MOVING

ON THE move all year long, the Masai, a nomadic people of east Africa, live mostly on the meat, blood, and milk of their herds. They stay in one place as long as the rain lasts. Natural ecologists, they leave an area before its resources are totally depleted, and return after the land has had time to recover.

Sadly, this aspect of the Masai lifestyle may soon be a thing of the past. Governments are encouraging the Masai to settle in one area. But they are herdsmen, not farmers. The grasslands they need are not easily bordered by fences and they have no tradition of planting or irrigation.[34]

Most of us do not farm or have herds that need grazing land. But we do live lives that sometimes deplete all the "resources" a particular job or position can give us. A time comes when we need to "move on."

We can each use a periodic evaluation. Every now and then, we need to look at what we are doing and ask ourselves if it isn't time to find a constructive way to move on to new challenges, a new position, or a new career. ♫

For in him we live and move and have our being.
—ACTS 17:28

STRESS LEVELS

HEALTH ACTIVISTS in Japan say that overwork kills 30,000 workers every year in that country. They even have a word for it—"karoshi." In America, 50 percent of all deaths each year are attributed to hypertension and stress-related illnesses.

A recent study of successful professionals revealed that they practiced stress-management techniques. Praying, walking on the beach, stroking the household pet, working out at the gym, or taking a long bubble bath all helped them to gain a sense of inner well-being and peace. The important point was not any one regimen, but that each person had discovered his or her own technique for relaxing.[35]

Jesus promised His disciples, "Peace I leave with you; my peace I give you. . . . Do not let your hearts be troubled and do not be afraid" (John 14:27). The inner peace Jesus gives us does not mean we will never experience conflict or difficulty. The peace that Jesus gives is the peace of reconciliation with God, unity with other Christians, and living at peace with the world around us. Within that peace, we still need creative ways of letting the stress melt away from our lives. We need to *learn* new ways to relax.

The work of righteousness shall be peace.
—ISAIAH 32:17 KJV

145

OFFERINGS

SAINT FRANCIS of Assisi was hoeing his garden one day when someone asked him what he would do if he were to learn that he was going to die before sunset on that very day. He replied, "I would finish hoeing my garden." Saint Francis saw all of his life as a sacrifice made to the Lord—an outpouring of his time, energy, and love that took many expressions, including his work. His life was a "direct" sacrifice.

Using the same analogy of a garden, Julian of Norwich pointed toward a second form of sacrifice:

Be a gardener.
Dig a ditch, toil and sweat,
and turn the earth upside down
and seek the deepness
and water the plants in time.
Continue this labor
and make sweet floods to run
and noble and abundant fruits to spring.
Take this food and drink
and carry it to God as your true worship.[36]

Consider the activities of your day and how they can be an offering of love and thanksgiving to the Lord. When we do all things for Him, even the most difficult tasks become a joy! ༄

May He remember all your meal offerings,
And find your burnt offering acceptable!
—Psalm 20:3 NASB

147

MAKE HAY WHILE
THE SUN SHINES

MEDICINE. WHAT a glamorous profession. High salaries, prestige, respect, travel, speaking engagements, curing the sick, discovering new drugs.

Medicine. Occasional tedium, exposure to a host of diseases, making an incorrect diagnosis, watching patients die, long hours, no sleep, no family time, malpractice suits.

Medicine. Maybe not so glamorous after all.

When a doctor spends most of the year trying to help her patients sort out various physical and mental ailments, while at the same time trying not to become too attached, where does she go to heal her own wounded spirit?

One doctor in Michigan goes back home to Vermont to help her father and brother with the haying. It's elegantly simple work, she says. Haying is hot, sweaty, tiring work, but it has a satisfying, beginning, middle, and end . . . unlike medicine.[37]

All of us need an activity that is the antithesis of what we do all day. We need a cobweb-clearer, a routine-shaker.

We each need to be completely out of our normal work mode for a little while every day—and for a week or two when we can manage it. It's a crucial part of living a *balanced* life! ᘐ

> *This is what the Lord says: "Stand at the crossroads and look;*
> *ask for the ancient paths, ask where the good way is,*
> *and walk in it, and you will find rest for your souls."*
> —JEREMIAH 6:16

THE CROWDED WAYS

ᗬ HENRY DAVID Thoreau once described the city as "a place where people are lonely together."

If Thoreau's observation was true in the past, it will become increasingly true in the present, and the prediction is that it will become alarmingly more so in the near future.

The hymn "Where Cross the Crowded Ways of Life" was written in 1903 by a Methodist minister pastoring in New York City. The words draw our attention to the mission field that exists in the cities where we live. They read in part:

Where cross the crowded ways of life, where sound the cries of race and clan, above the noise of selfish strife, we hear Thy voice, O Son of man!

The cup of water giv'n for Thee still holds the freshness of Thy grace; yet long these multitudes to see the sweet compassion of Thy face.

O Master, from the mountain side, make haste to heal these hearts of pain; among these restless throngs abide; O tread the city streets again:

Till sons of men shall learn Thy love and follow where Thy feet have trod; till glorious, from Thy heav'n above, shall come the city of our God.[38] ✍

Defend the poor and fatherless: do justice to the afflicted and needy.
Deliver the poor and needy: rid them out of the hand of the wicked.
—PSALM 82:3-4 KJV

DAILY BREAD

WHEN JESUS instituted the Last Supper, He told His disciples to "do this in remembrance of me." Remembering something or someone is to allow that thing or person to shape and influence our life. When we go to the Lord's Table, we give witness to the fact we are depending upon Jesus.

As we remember Jesus, we have the picture of Him giving himself to us to nurture and feed our souls. A song written by Arden Autry describes Jesus' total self-giving to us:

As you eat this bread, as you drink this cup,
let your heart give thanks and be lifted up.
Your soul can rest in this truth secure:
As you eat this bread, all I am is yours.

All I am is yours. All I am I gave,
dying on the cross, rising from the grave,
your sins to bear and your life restore:
As you eat this bread, all I am is yours.

In delight and joy, in the depths of pain,
in the anxious hours, through all loss and gain,
your world may shake, but my Word endures:
As you eat this bread, all I am is yours.[39]

We do not have a High Priest who cannot sympathize with our weaknesses,
but was in all points tempted as we are, yet without sin.
—HEBREWS 4:15 NKJV

ENDNOTES

1. *Illustrations for Preaching & Teaching*, Craig B. Larson, (Grand Rapids, MI: Baker Book House, 1993), p. 187.

2. *Guide to Prayer for All God's People*, Rueben P. Job and Norman Shawchuck, ed. (Nashville: Upper Room, 1990), pp. 255-256.

3. *Illustrations Unlimited*, James S. Hewett, ed. (Wheaton: Tyndale House, 1988), p. 19.

4. *Good Housekeeping*, February 1996, p. 20.

5. *Encyclopedia Judaica*, Prof. Cecil Roth and Dr. Geoffrey Wigoder, eds. (Jerusalem: Kefer Publishing House, 1972), Vol. 4, pp. 142-143.

6. *Illustrations for Preaching & Teaching*, Craig B. Larson (Grand Rapids, MI: Baker Book House, 1993), p. 106.

7. *Spiritual Fitness*, Doris Donnelly (San Francisco: Harper, 1993), pp. 111-124.

8. "Leisure," *The Family Book of Best Loved Poems*, David L. George, ed. (Garden City, NY: Doubleday & Co., 1952), p. 261.

9. *JAMA*, December 6, 1995, p. 21.

10. *Illustrations for Preaching & Teaching*, Craig B. Larson (Grand Rapids, MI: Baker Book House, 1993), p. 122.

11. Ibid., p. 190.

12. *I Like This Poem*, Kaye Webb, ed. (Middlesex, England: Penguin Books, 1979), pp. 156-157.

13. *The Treasure Chest*, Brian Culhane, ed. (San Francisco: Harper, 1995), p. 162.

14. *Illustrations Unlimited*, James S. Hewett (Wheaton, IL: Tyndale House Publishers, 1988), p. 40.

15. Ibid., p. 389.

16. *Treasury of the Christian Faith*, Stanley Stuber and Thomas Clark, ed. (NY: Association Press, 1949), p. 355.

17. *The Treasure Chest*, Brian Culhane, ed. (San Francisco: Harper, 1995), p. 162.

18. Ibid., p. 171.

19. *Knight's Master Book of 4,000 Illustrations*, Walter B. Knight (Grand Rapids, MI: William B. Eerdmans Publishing Co., 1956), p. 64.

20. Ibid., p. 71.

21. *Illustrations Unlimited*, James S. Hewett, ed. (Wheaton: Tyndale House, 1988), pp. 15, 18, 279-280.

22. *Newsweek*, March 6, 1995, pp. 60-61.

23. *The Treasure Chest*, Brian Culhane, ed., (San Francisco: Harper, 1995), p. 171.

24. *God's Song in My Heart*, Ruth Youngdahl Nelson (Philadelphia: Fortress Press, 1957), pp. 248-249.

25. *Scientific American*, October 1995, p. 50.

26. Ibid., August 1995, p. 70-77.

27. *The Treasure Chest*, Brian Culhane, ed., (San Francisco: Harper, 1995), p. 188.

28. *A Guide to Prayer for All God's People*, Rueben P. Job and Norman Shawchuck, ed. (Nashville: Upper Room Books, 1990), pp. 326-328.

29. *Westways*, March 1996, pp. 19-21.

30. *The Treasure Chest*, Brian Culhane, ed., (San Francisco: Harper, 1995), p. 200.

31. *Knight's Master Book of 4,000 Illustrations*, Walter B. Knight (Grand Rapids, MI: William B. Eerdmans Publishing Co., 1956), p. 615.

32. *Lord, Let Me Love*, Marjorie Holmes (NY: Doubleday, [date]), pp. 104-105.

33. *Amazing Grace*, Kenneth W. Osbeck (Grand Rapids, MI: Kregel Publications, 1990), p. 38.

34. *Scientific American*, January 1994, p. 159.

35. *Newsweek*, March 6, 1995, p. 62.

36. *The Treasure Chest*, Brian Culhane, ed. (San Francisco: Harper, 1995), p. 204.

37. *JAMA*, January 10, 1996, p. 99.

38. *Amazing Grace*, Kenneth W. Osbeck (Grand Rapids, MI: Kregel Publications, 1990), p. 324.

39. Song used with permission of Arden Autry.

Additional copies of this book and other titles
in the *Quiet Moments with God* series
are available from your local bookstore.

Breakfast with God, clothbound devotional
Breakfast with God, portable
Coffee Break with God, clothbound devotional
Coffee Break with God, portable
Tea Time with God, clothbound devotional
Sunset with God, clothbound devotional

Honor Books
Tulsa, Oklahoma